Model Poet

Poetry by:
Rebecca L. Bonham

Model Poet
Copyright ©2021 Rebecca Bonham
Cover Art: William (Beejay) Jackson

All rights reserved. Blue Jade Press, LLC retains the right to reprint this book. Permission to reprint poems from this collection must be obtained by the author.

ISBN- 978-1-7333822-6-7

Published by:

Blue Jade Press, LLC

Blue Jade Press, LLC
Vineland, NJ 08360
www.bluejadepress.com

Acknowledgements

I can hear the Academy Awards in the background as I think of all the people that should be thanked and recognized for continuously supporting my dreams.

Thank you to my parents for allowing me to question everything, to learn from my mistakes and being the lifeline when I needed to return to center. To my siblings John, Katie, Freddy, Megan and Allison, without you, I wouldn't have as many stories or be as tough as I am. Thank you for the lifetime of silliness.

Jackie, I was unsure if I should put you with family, but you chose to be my lifelong friend. From high school to starting our own business, you've always had my back, thank you for always being there (even when I'm wrong).

Beejay, thank you for suggesting that I write this book 15 years ago and listening to me fuss over it for as long. Hey look…here it is… and the cover is amazing.

Adam, thank you for listening to every new poem and being my +1 to every open mic I can find.

Thank you to Millville Art's District and all those who attend Resurgence Open Mic. You encourage me to step into the spotlight and live my dream. Your love and acceptance is tangible and keeps me uplifted. Linda, Rich, Diane, Maryann, Jesse, Bob, Kim, Sara… Thank you.

I could read a million poems and not find the inspiration that I've found in my poet friends. Thank you for pushing me to write, to publish this book, and believing in me. Rita, Bob, Ryan, John, Anthony, Barry, Todd, Kate, Alma, and Renee… I have the best bookshelf.

To my husband Kevin thank you for making me feel safe to process and write the poems in this book and for supporting my poetry even though sometimes you don't understand it.

Alex, my son, all of it has been for you. Thank you for making each day worth it.

The following poems have been previously published

"Piercing" L'Spirit, Cumberland Co. College, 2007
"Hostess" Disorder II Red Dashboard LLC, 2017
"Theatre of War" Moving beyond Mars, Red Dashboard LLC, 2018.

To my little man…

Table of Contents

Dandelions	1
Health Advocacy	3
The Boy I Graduated Next To	5
Temporary	6
Industrial Sand	7
Inherited	8
Theatre of War	10
@$#&!!!!!	12
The Other Side	13
Singed	15
A Judicial Fight	16
Solid	17
Penance	18
1999	19
As Seen on TV	20
A Grave Spring	21
Ping	22
City Tears	23
Eulogy	24
The Drowned	25
Ghosted	26
Building Blocks	27
Slipping	28
Super Star	29
Model Poet	30
Unseen	31
Weight	32
Silhouette	33
Hostess	34

Inept Empath	35
Absurd	36
Tonight	37
Midnight Musing	39
Self-Depleting	41
Adjustment Needed	42
Windshield Meditation	43
Piercing	44
Garage Zen	45
Sight	46
Tuned In	47
Life is Good (At Shalom Cemetery)	48

Dandelions

As the sunny crowns
broke through the frozen ground
An opportunity presented itself
to an enterprising seven-year-old
A spade and a bucket
each dandelion dug
was a quarter in my pocket
I set upon the neighbor's yard
and delicately freed each one
containing all the early fluff
(Which in hindsight lessened my profit)

I was approached by the neighbor boy
who, being ten, was so much wiser
and was confused by my industry
He decided on a quicker way
and started pulling them from the stems
and blowing all the fluff
All protests resulted in
the smearing of pollen
yellow streaks under my chin

Then came the dare
of course I was to go first
to eat the poisonous blossom
and bite and chew the fluff
After I thought,
something that tasted that awful
must be deadly and now
I'm surrounded by the sickly smell.

This day was my last
I didn't heed the warnings
of eating things that grew wild outside
or trusting the intentions of little boys
That night I behaved angelically
kissing my parents goodbye
for tonight, this seven-year-old
thought surely that she'd die

The Boy I Graduated Next To

8th grade angst, big-dog, hair bands
Listening to the Beasties and the Cure
Classes and field trips, oral reports,
air-conditioned Apple II e
Hot summer field day, egg drop physics
Poetry assignment bogus school spirt
Baloney won, Read out LOUD?!
Everyone, auditorium
Freak out, I'm the quiet one!
He said, "Mine's bogus too"

12th grade resignation work and school
Clubs, and creative writing turned into:
Adulting classes, home finance, typing,
and Pascal
Insecure, and too mature to want to party
Starting work and life the next day,
nothing exciting
Confusion of my classmates' cheer.
Not a new beginning, just what's next.
He said, "I don't feel it. Do you?"

Temporary

Lived between two homes
A suitcase every other weekend
I moved eighteen times
All within the same county

Possessions are weaknesses
Emotion infused relics
Easily broken
Unlike will or fortitude
Fragility exploited and exposed
With glued cracks

Trash bags, stuffed with necessities
Shoved in a trunk that symbolized
Freedom on four bald tires
Remnants that survived my past.

Industrial Sand

Ancient factories built on sugar sand
Abundant commodity to glass
Blazing furnaces
Firing soda-pop bottles
Replaced by petroleum
Closing... sand shifts
Converting to test tubes
Plastics inserts
Repeating piecework
Counting the hours in cents
Sand shifts again
Then pounds and euros
Sold across the sea
Lay-offs, double shifts
The sand shifts... Closed

Inherited

I come from Lyons
A lineage of trials and endurance
A midwife left Wales
and married and English businessman
Who believed in trains and planes
and mail and supplies to Ireland
Who liked pretty secretaries
and brought one home
to live with his wife
When she railed against
moving his mistress in
he had her committed
to the sanitarium

But I come from Lyons
as did she
and she persevered until
the short fragile peace
between warring worlds
and won her own divorce

Lyons do not belong
on trains nor planes
or caged in sanitariums
So she returned to Wales
to continue her midwifery
and lived a life of solitude
until she finally won
her personal war of tenacity
and passed away aged 103.

Theatre of War

I've been ordered home.
The ceasefire has ended.
There will be a chain reaction.
Darkened streets and locked doors
accompany me home: Gunshots,
backfires, raised voices, sirens, unease,
Danger

Check for improvised weapons in my
purse:
Scissors, keys, books.
Ambushed at the front door.
Firearms, k-bars, pregnant chokeholds, a
view down the Barrel, no escape.

My baby cries.
Turning into: promises, pleas, diffusion,
tears, apologies, flowers
Home, soon demolished- condemned
After paying last month's rent.

Last day, payday, fermented liquid
check, drunken excuses, last straw.
Laying on the bed grappling,
He has the upper hand:
Eye-gouging, name-calling: whore, cunt,
privileged one.

This time
No weapons, fair fight, adrenalin hit,
mule kick,
Broken furniture, hurdle the gate
Grab the phone and the baby

Escape.

@$#&!!!!

The Devil you say?
An imaginary friend to lay blame your offense.

I own my offenses.
There is a litany of them, for which I am judged.

The Other Side

The other side
When tenderness gave way
To vodka fueled rage
When I rushed into the pit
Embraced the violence
Dared you to follow
Where upon the pyre
I placed your music box
Danced naked to the dying notes
Of words that should have been said.
I am not a requiem

I gathered my spirits
Left through the back door
Shunned by the black light
Diminished in your shadows
Sober and faded
I chose a different path
Filled with shame and remorse
With the hope to feel again
I became a ghost

I am not a muse
Cast in the leading role
Of your poetic lament
Nor a page you turn to in regret
A reminder of your life ill spent
Just a character you revisit
And pick the other choice

I pray I never become a poem
After you find your voice.

Singed

You were always good with romance.
Your dreams were all within my
imagination, and wrapped in your arms.
You only come to me when low,
burning with desire.
You are hungry, for the simple comfort
  of my lap.
You hide your fears from reality as a
  petted child.
Whose worries can only be lifted by my
  simple grace.
Then when refreshed by my presence,
and, sated by the passion you inspire;
you recede, taking my peace and
creativity.
When I have had all the sorrow,
I can bear, you wake
and the adoration fades
from your face.
Leaving me with your woes and cares.
You fail at ever after.

A Judicial Fight

I am worried,
because I trust not in the system.
I am worried, because he is stronger in
his hate than I am.

My anger grows, pushing me to be
someone I abhor.
My patience for karma is fading.
I am caged and fearful to fight.
He has so much more practice.

Solid

You stood above me
And compressed me
And pressed me
Sent your roots
To leech
Divinity
As you bloomed and bore fruit

Penance

I walked into the sunrise
Taking the short path
As east as I could go
Until my feet touched sand
And the familiar crunch
Of tumbled shells.

I stood in the stillness
A maelstrom in my mind
Felt the ocean free the earth
From beneath my toes
I expect the withdrawal
And follow the tide

I wade into the undertow
Burying my calves in the sand
Switching into an inferno
Forming my resolve
Daring Llyr to summon me
And pull me past the swells

I turn my back and look ashore
Allow the breakers to pummel my back
Fearless in my feigned courage
Safe in my childish defiance
My preferred form of penance
My sun baked test of will.

1999

I think I'd like to stay
In your memory
Where I'll always be
Twenty-two

As Seen on TV

I don't have to imagine
The perfect time lapse image
Of a gun aimed at the temple
The slow motion bullet
Leaving in a black burst
The perfect concave of flesh ruined
By penetration

I don't have to imagine
The sting of rubber
The clenching of fists
The puncture of a plump vein
The release
Flushed flesh turned wax

I don't have to imagine
A bathroom filled with candles
Wine and prescriptions scattered
Tepid water tinged red
The slow drip
Soaking the floorboards
Hesitant cuts against blue flesh

I sit in warmth and quiet
Watching the screen
Tasting copper pennies
Smelling decay
Listening to the drips
Wishing I had to imagine.

A Grave Spring

I awoke to the dropping of pink petals
amid the grey stones.
Woken too soon by the explosions of
yellow, underscored by fields of purple.
I lie in this place of cold, death, sadness.

The barest of branches dare to bud,
by the warming of the false spring sun.
I wept when the winds whipped
the broken branches of the willows,
adding to the dead.

Believing my peace, my place, the same.
My shadow no longer shone, but
violently tossed against the upturned
stones, your sentiments skewed.

Ping

Has it come to this
….
A ping
….
A hey from a friend
…..
No words no ring just text
….
No soothing voices to soften the blow
….
An old friend has died
….
Do you remember him
….
Such a tragedy…

City Tears

I wept for the chaos
churning me, burning me
leaving me standing on the sidewalk
looking at the multicolored chalk lines of
your soul.

They float spinning me, dipping me,
sweeping my hair across the rain-washed
gutters.
Dripping, I stand to wipe
the sandy gray drops from my chest,
where they cling to my shirt,
reminding me of you.

Eulogy

It was that absence of noise,
I never knew it was there.
Sound screams at you,
For me, they are dull and faded
Faintly echoing the laughter of the
 past.
I fail to grasp those echoes
Happiness slips from my fingers,
leaving a mess of me.

The Drowned

She reaches in and pulls out the drowned
noticing the frozen expression
of acceptance,
pearlescent complexion
laid upon the ground.
oozing what once sustained
the sea reclaims

She watches
the tide take, sun bake,
and the sand beat
the acceptance from her face.

Ghosted

Softly I tread on glass so broken
Miles of words left unspoken
I kneel and weep, knees left bloody,
My will is weak, my vision muddy.
I will rise and face my goals
To continue on with hardened soles.

Building Blocks

We build our foundations
on grains of sand
understanding an imposing moon
or violent sea could shift our existence

Our homes constructed
of ancient scrub pines
stilts sunk deep past the water line
we turn our commodity to glass

Fragile industry exists
on shifting ground
our castles built not of stone or clouds
but of sand.

Slipping

I take up too much room
So I search for the cracks
Where I can pour myself like sand
Stretched and disconnected
Around immovable objects
Thinking time and grit
Will win me my place
But as I wear down stone
It becomes polished
The sand slips
Unable to retain its form
Held up by purpose for so long

Super Star

I shy from the spotlight
I like to see you fill it
more comfortable behind the curtains
treasuring each step that lead you onto
the stage.

Hidden from the applause
I watch them worship you
joyful in knowing
they see what I do.

Model Poet

I sit exposed and centered in easels
bubbling with deep seated fears
I'm perfectly still
ten, one minute poses
for these, I listen to my body

Feel the fatigue of the exaggerated
  stretch
I hear feverish sketching
but the screaming in my limbs
demands my attention

Relief brings a smile and a chat
"I'm a poet, a fill in, a friend"
then I settle into a posed meditation
eyes open and with blurred sight I
wonder

As they draw my lines,
my negative space
and remove my clothing with their pens
Do they see the poem that is forming?
The poem is what is real

Scribbling, painting, tapping of brushes
a furious soundtrack to which
I imagine they are filling their pages
with my poetry, my words, my energy
the rest is but a shell

Unseen

Did you know I was there?
When you dropped your composure
and the weight of your mask
You recognized my language
and spoke of Ezra instead

You showed me every wound
challenged me to retch
contradicted acceptance
I showed you mine
all the places that still bled

I raged against your chest
and bounced off your walls
in inflated lunacy, daring you
but in the silence
where volumes are written and read
marble becomes flesh.

Weight

Standing behind him
in stocking feet and a satin shift
he drops his shoulders
I notice the weight as I lift his coat,
needing both hands
to gently return it to its wooden hanger

He has already loosened the knot
that guards his words.
With shaking fingers, I try
to work, the buttons down his chest
Each one reminding me
of how easy it is
to walk out of my dress.

Silhouette

Drawn as a silhouette on the moon
my shadowed existence endures
seen as only a reflection
in the passing glow
hazy red whispers of my presence
but, for a glimpse, a passing notion
was I even there?

Hostess

Do you feel that sense of calm
when you walk into my house?
That is me.
The energy I give off,
while absorbing all of yours.
You take from me without knowing.

You give me your woes,
your fears, your anger.
I bear them
on the narrow shoulders of
my ego.

Devouring them, bite by vile bite,
smiling in the process.
Pleasant conversation through the
nauseated pain of carrying your load.

Enjoy your calm, your peace, your
serenity, for it costs me so.

Inept Empath

You ask me what I see.
you say I have witches' sight.
I see faded, water stained, snapshots,
filled with apparitions and energy
you demand answers;
you simply have to know

"Go ahead. Do It, Tell me"
anxiety chases the gift
so sorry, it's gone
now, I am a blind seer, who gives fickle
 fortunes
I am not a lens; I cannot be adjusted.
I am only the carrier, the express
but, you want answers
from this inept empath.
Yet, I have not looked inside.
The wax is brittle and the seam is dry.

Absurd

As I listen to you,
I think of the edible balloon.
I taste the apple and caramel,
Breathing in the sweet lightness of
helium.

Constricted,
I let loose a falsetto titter.
Amused by the absurdity of it all.

Tonight

This night, not unlike many others
I worry
of things I said, or didn't say
of how I could have been kinder...
better... more

I believe
that I walk through my life invisible
but somehow judged by strangers
and found wanting

I struggle
With a sense of self
an internal dialogue
that reads between the lines
that aren't double spaced
Sorting excitement from anxiety
wondering which came first

I wrestle
For the need of obscurity
and the desire for recognition
fearing and craving both
But tonight, is not unlike many others
So in this I wonder
if it's enough

To put ink to pen
pen to paper
and scratch your thoughts hard enough
to press them out of my head
Out of my soul.

Midnight Musing

I allow myself
to leave my body
only after I wind
the roots around my form
tuck it in with angel wings
and fly away leaving myself

At first I tip toed
in my ghostly form
down he darkened hallway
places well known
then floated o'er the stone floor
and subsequently out the door.

With the world before me
where do I dare to go?
Travel to the unknown?
Do I give into fantasies?
Do I meditate?
Find my sense of self?

I imagine my nightmares
of a somewhat familiar house
that exists only in my dreams.
Do I dare to face the horrors
in my ethereal form?

I decide to wander
and anger myself
finding futility and indecision
unable to find purpose
wasting this experience
far too involved with earthly concerns

I find myself
returning to my body
viewing it with scorn
I find it to be the symbol
of all the lessons
I've failed to learn.

Self-depleting

I cannot draw a stick
I cannot sing a note
All I have to offer
Is this crap I wrote.

Adjustment Needed

I feel affinity for the shut in
I've felt the slowing of life
that is required for the endurance
of all things

I'm unsure what it is to hunker
but I can physically feel
my soul lowering
getting heavy
perhaps adjusting its center of gravity
to lean into the endless waves
of other people's feelings

Years upon years of trying not to feel
and never understanding
how not to care instead
not care enough to stand
to ease the tension
from the hips and thighs
to remember that you can stiffen
in your fighting stance

Windshield Meditation

Alone in my thoughts
I start to believe
if I drive long enough
I could see myself
on this road before

Piercing

Light comes in an instant
Piercing through my closed eyes
The dancing lights amuse me
As I try to wake
The events of my dreams
Roll through my mind
I turn over to escape
The light is relentless,
Nudging and prodding
"Wake up, wake up!" it screams to me.
"Too much to see, that is not within!"
"Yesterday's accounts are tallied"
"Your data recorded and revised"
At last. I succumb, folding away my dreams
To wake to life's certainty.

Garage Zen

Supine meditation in the cinderblock
  cathedral
Amid the gasoline aromatherapy
Worries buzz and bite leaving
Itchy reminders of bad decisions
Anxiety driven ambition
Aches from a body too tired
To run at the speed of thought

Sight

I looked inward
and blamed all problems on myself
retracing each step
that may have broken stride
with the equilibrium of how things
are supposed to be

Tuned in

I feel the energy in every cell.
each one with its own hammer and anvil
drumming in unison

To walk is to master the beat
the unchangeable, the core
sway with the rhythm of age

Relaxing into wisdom
tip toeing through the melodies
the short-lived and most remembered

But the story floats about
drifting, slipping eluding my grasp
it leaves me with empty words
full of thought

Mood changes, the words blur
shifting, cascading, tumbling
on themselves

Words become beat and rhythm
pulsing, driving, demanding
to be formed

Life is Good
(at Shalom Cemetery)

Every March I itch
peering hopefully at my forsythia
begging for the yellow blooms
that say it's ok, it's time, they're ready.
They're already here.
And, when they opened today
I went for my 15th spring walk
through Shalom Cemetery

OPEN DAWN TIL DUSK
NO DOGS ALLOWED

I cross the street and pass the sign
(which looks newly painted)
I should know,
last fall I thought,
(like me)
it was just hanging on
to the stone pillar that
keeps the dead in
(and dogs out)

I immediately turn right
The living here have rules
(or at least I do)
There are stops I must make
for people I've only met
after they ended up here

Alexander is the first
his spirit called to me
when I happened upon his friend
sitting, sobbing in futility
I, out for a walk empty hands
asked if I could assist
He needed more than matches
to light his lantern, in memory
I pulled a lighter from my bra
and hugged poor Alex's friend
and cried with him as it floated away
I stop now for Alexander and check in

A quick trip around the loop
There are no children today
learning how to skate and ride
with bright helmets and pads
and new bicycles and nervous parents
None of that today, this section is sad
this year I walk solemnly
around too many fresh graves

I taught my own Alexander how to ride
(and later how to drive)
through the safe winding paths
pedal past though the back part
past the chapel in the shade and shadows
past the spooky stone
where it's always cold
I wonder if those buried there
have seen how much he's grown.

Around the chapel to the sunny side
the dead make themselves known
I find inspiration and poems happen here
and another stop in my determined stride
I like to stand under the dripping blooms
of the willow trees
to say hi to Mary,
(who I only recently found)
Last year there was a placard
outlining her life
She was a publisher, author
as well as a mother and a Civil War
soldier's wife.
I like to stop and reflect
on our similarities.

Onto to the other side
(where serious walkers and runners go)
There are rules for the living
and down the long stretch
not even the oak trees grow
rows and rows of family stones
(this is the busiest part)
I try to avoid the grieving
(and the kids smoking pot)

The final leg and I start to run
I always pick up my pace
before I get to the Veterans' stones
I like to think when I'm sweaty and
 winded

I hear them cheer me on.
I stop to straighten the fallen flags
for those that fell too soon

It's a neutral day a Shalom Cemetery
no laughter or sorrow
from the living or the dead
just a gift of rebirth and inspiration
as I pass back through
the iron gates

Rebecca Bonham is a lifelong resident of Southern New Jersey. After years of hosting and attending open mics, she continues her love of art and literature as co-owner of Blue Jade Press, LLC. In her spare time, she's adjusting to being an empty-nester with her husband, two dogs, and many plants.

www.ingramcontent.com/pod-product-compliance
Lightning Source LLC
Chambersburg PA
CBHW071756040426
42446CB00012B/2589